Major European
Union Nations

MAJOR EUROPEAN UNION NATIONS

Austria
Belgium
Czech Republic
Denmark
France
Germany
Greece
Ireland

Italy
The Netherlands
Poland
Portugal
Spain
Sweden
United Kingdom

Major European Union Nations

GREECE

by
Kim Etingoff and Shaina C. Indovino

Mason Crest

Mason Crest
370 Reed Road, Broomall,
Pennsylvania 19008
www.masoncrest.com

Printed in the Hashemite Kingdom of Jordan.

First printing
9 8 7 6 5 4 3 2 1

Library of Congress Cataloging-in-Publication Data

Etingoff, Kim.
  Greece / by Kim Etingoff and Shaina C. Indovino.
      p. cm. — (The European Union: political, social, and economic cooperation)
  Includes index.
  ISBN 978-1-4222-2244-7 (hardcover) — ISBN 978-1-4222-2231-7 (series hardcover) — ISBN 978-1-4222-9268-6 (ebook)
  1. Greece—Juvenile literature. I. Indovino, Shaina Carmel. II. Title.
  DF717.E752 2012
  949.5—dc22
                                    2010051304

Produced by Harding House Publishing Services, Inc.
www.hardinghousepages.com
Interior layout by Micaela Sanna.
Cover design by Torque Advertising + Design.

CONTENTS

INTRODUCTION 8

1. MODERN ISSUES 11

2. GREECE'S HISTORY AND GOVERNMENT 17

3. THE ECONOMY 27

4. GREECE'S PEOPLE AND CULTURE 37

5. LOOKING TO THE FUTURE 47

TIME LINE 54

FURTHER READING/INTERNET RESOURCES 56

FOR MORE INFORMATION 58

GLOSSARY 59

INDEX 62

PICTURE CREDITS 63

ABOUT THE AUTHOR AND THE CONSULTANT 64

GREECE

European Union Member since 1981

Dráma ●   Xánthi ●   ● Komotiní

Sirrhae ●

Kavála ●

Thessaloníki ●

● Kastoría

Kérkyra ●

Lárisa

● Ioánnina   ●

Trikala   Vólos
         ●

Lamia ●

● Agrínion

Chalcis ●

Peiraiéfs ●
  ★ Athens

● Pátrai

● Kalámai

Chaniá ●   Irákleton ●

INTRODUCTION

Sixty years ago, Europe lay scarred from the battles of the Second World War. During the next several years, a plan began to take shape that would unite the countries of the European continent so that future wars would be inconceivable. On May 9, 1950, French Foreign Minister Robert Schuman issued a declaration calling on France, Germany, and other European countries to pool together their coal and steel production as "the first concrete foundation of a European federation." "Europe Day" is celebrated each year on May 9 to commemorate the beginning of the European Union (EU).

The EU consists of twenty-seven countries, spanning the continent from Ireland in the west to the border of Russia in the east. Eight of the ten most recently admitted EU member states are former communist regimes that were behind the Iron Curtain for most of the latter half of the twentieth century.

Any European country with a democratic government, a functioning market economy, respect for fundamental rights, and a government capable of implementing EU laws and policies may apply for membership. Bulgaria and Romania joined the EU in 2007. Croatia, Serbia, Turkey, Iceland, Montenegro, and Macedonia have also embarked on the road to EU membership.

While the EU began as an idea to ensure peace in Europe through interconnected economies, it has evolved into so much more today:

- Citizens can travel freely throughout most of the EU without carrying a passport and without stopping for border checks.

- EU citizens can live, work, study, and retire in another EU country if they wish.

- The euro, the single currency accepted throughout seventeen of the EU countries (with more to come), is one of the EU's most tangible achievements, facilitating commerce and making possible a single financial market that benefits both individuals and businesses.

- The EU ensures cooperation in the fight against cross-border crime and terrorism.

- The EU is spearheading world efforts to preserve the environment.

- As the world's largest trading bloc, the EU uses its influence to promote fair rules for world trade, ensuring that globalization also benefits the poorest countries.

- The EU is already the world's largest donor of humanitarian aid and development assistance, providing around 60 percent of global official development assistance to developing countries in 2011.

The EU is not a nation intended to replace existing nations. The EU is unique—its member countries have established common institutions to which they delegate some of their sovereignty so that decisions on matters of joint interest can be made democratically at the European level.

Europe is a continent with many different traditions and languages, but with shared values such as democracy, freedom, and social justice, cherished values well known to North Americans. Indeed, the EU motto is "United in Diversity."

Enjoy your reading. Take advantage of this chance to learn more about Europe and the EU!

Ambassador John Bruton,
Former EU President and Prime Minister of Ireland

Athens City, Greece

CHAPTER 1 MODERN ISSUES

Life is hard for the average person in Greece these days. Joanna Panagioto, a volunteer at a community web radio station, told her story to the UK *Guardian*:

Since coming back to Greece I've had two short temporary contracts. I've been unemployed since July 2010 and have sent 300 CVs with no luck (including for positions in a warehouse or on a shop floor). In the meantime I've managed to earn some cash by doing random odd jobs, but it's devastating and disheartening when you're unemployed because you're forced to live with your parents, unable to make plans for the future. Having said that, I guess it must have been a shock for my generation—I am 32—as we were raised with a career mindset, and now since everything has turned upside down we are working merely to survive. I would be lying if I said I am not considering leaving Greece again.

The Formation of the European Union

The EU is a confederation of European nations that continues to grow. All countries that enter the EU agree to follow common laws about foreign security policies. They also agree to cooperate on legal matters that go on within the EU. The European Council meets to discuss all international matters and make decisions about them. Each country's own concerns and interests are important, though. And apart from legal and financial issues, the EU tries to uphold values such as peace and solidarity, human dignity, freedom, and equality. All member countries remain autonomous. This means that they generally keep their own laws and regulations. The EU becomes involved only if there is an international issue or if a member country has violated the principles of the union.

The idea for a union among European nations was first mentioned after World War II. The war had devastated much of Europe, both physically and financially. In 1950, French foreign minister Robert Schuman suggested that France and West Germany combine their coal and steel industries under one authority. Both countries would have control over the industries. This would help them become more financially stable. It would also make war between the countries much more difficult. The idea was interesting to other European countries as well. In 1951, France, West Germany, Belgium, Luxembourg, the Netherlands, and Italy signed the Treaty of Paris, creating the European Coal and Steel Community. These six countries would become the core of the EU.

In 1957, these same countries signed the Treaties of Rome, creating the European Economic Community. This combined their economies into a single European economy. In 1965, the Merger Treaty brought together a number of these treaty organizations. The organizations were joined under a common banner, known as the European Community. Finally, in 1992, the Maastricht Treaty was signed. This treaty defined the European Union. It gave a framework for expanding the EU's political role, particularly in the area of foreign and security policy. It would also replace national currencies with the euro. The next year, the treaty went into effect. At that time, the member countries included the original six plus another six who had joined during the 1970s and '80s.

In the following years, the EU would take more steps to form a single market for its members. This would make joining the union even more of an advantage. Three more countries joined during the 1990s. Another twelve joined in the first decade of the twenty-first century. As of 2012, six countries were waiting to join the EU.

The EU has made difficult decisions in order to save the Greek economy and protect other nations from economic disaster, but not all member states are eager to spend money on aid to struggling economies.

Joanna's story isn't that unusual for someone living in her country. All eyes have been on Greece in recent years—and unfortunately, people haven't generally been casting a generous glance at this Mediterranean country. Greece has been the hardest hit country during the recent economic *recession*. Its problems have spilled over to other countries, especially those in the European Union.

Starting in 2009, it became clear that Greece was spending too much money. When the global economy stalled that year, Greece was soon in trouble.

Greece and a handful of other EU nations are still facing some hard times. However, because Greece is in the EU, it can count on other members to help out. Greece is critically in debt. In response, the EU has offered the country new loans totaling billions of dollars. So far, the EU has given Greece two extremely large bailout packages—one for $147 billion and a second for $169 billion.

This is one of the first real tests facing the EU. Can it hold itself together? Can all the member states work together to help out those that are struggling? Greece is a major test of European unity.

REACTIONS IN GREECE

Meanwhile, the average Greek citizen isn't concerned with what is going on at such a large scale. Greece's economic problems have meant big changes for the Greek people, for their everyday lives. The government no longer has money to provide things like schooling, retirement benefits, and health care the way it used to.

Greeks have not responded well to these changes. There have been protests, strikes, and general unrest. Labor unions and public trans-

The economic crisis in Greece has driven citizens to the streets to protest cuts in government spending on social programs.

portation workers have gone on strike, causing major disruptions. Taxis, trains, buses, and subways have screeched to a halt as workers took to the street to protest.

There are lots of things to protest, at least from the point of view of the average Greek. Government workers are being laid off. Health care, education, and other important institutions are facing big cuts. One in eight people are unemployed. Taxes are being raised.

On May 5, 2010, three people were killed in a protest. They were trapped inside a bank that was set on fire. The protest started out peacefully, but turned violent, as protestor threw bombs and police responded with tear gas and pepper spray.

Greece is in trouble. Despite that, it has a long and proud history that continues to give its people strength and a sense of identity. It will need to draw on that strength in order to survive the challenges it faces in the twenty-first century.

Greece has a long and ancient history

2 GREECE'S HISTORY AND GOVERNMENT

CHAPTER

Greece's ancient history is familiar to many students in the Western word, but historians often debate just when the period referred to as "Ancient Greece" began. Some say it began with the first Olympic Games in 776 BCE, and some include the **prehistoric** Minoans and Mycanaeans as part of Ancient Greece. However, Ancient Greece is now usually acknowledged to have begun around 1000 BCE.

Greece's history is important to the history of the world. Greek culture influenced the later Roman Empire, which in turn directly affected Western Europe and the Americas. In order to understand Western society's beginnings, it is important to understand Greek society.

PREHISTORIC GREECE

What is now modern-day Greece was originally inhabited by a group of people known as the Minoans. The earliest recorded sign that the Minoans lived on the Balkan Peninsula dates to approximately 3000 BCE. These people were peace-loving traders who established ties with other civilizations around the world.

Around 1600 BCE, the Minoans were overtaken by a new group, the Mycenaeans. These people brought the beginning of the **Bronze Age** with them, which lasted until 1100 BCE. Decorative arts flourished, and the stage was set for later mythological writings meant to have taken place during this time. Mysteriously, the Mycenaean civilization was destroyed. Some **archaeologists** believe an invasion by the Dorians, with their superior weapons made of iron, destroyed the Mycenaean civilization.

ANCIENT DARK AGES

Whatever caused the downfall of the Mycenaeans, Greece entered a dark age. Population declined, as did education and the literacy rate. Even the language stopped being written. Cities were looted and destroyed, or abandoned and never rebuilt. Art such as pottery and jewelry lacked the **intricacy** of earlier times. The trade that had grown under the Minoans and Mycenaeans died out.

As Greece slowly emerged from this dark period, culture and civilization began to reemerge. Toward the end of the Dark Ages, **Phoenicians** reintroduced writing to the Grecians. Homer then wrote his **epics** and other writers recorded the oral history of the time.

DATING SYSTEMS AND THEIR MEANING

You might be accustomed to seeing dates expressed with the abbreviations BC or AD, as in the year 1000 BC or the year AD 1900. For centuries, this dating system has been the most common in the Western world. However, since BC and AD are based on Christianity (BC stands for Before Christ and AD stands for *anno Domini*, Latin for "in the year of our Lord"), many people now prefer to use abbreviations that people from all religions can be comfortable using. The abbreviations BCE (meaning Before Common Era) and CE (meaning Common Era) mark time in the same way (for example, 1000 BC is the same year as 1000 BCE, and AD 1900 is the same year as 1900 CE), but BCE and CE do not have the same religious overtones as BC and AD.

OFFICIAL ANCIENT GREECE: LEARNING AND WAR

The city-state (the *polis*) rose in significance during the ancient days of Greece. The two most famous were Athens and Sparta, centers of learning and advancements, although there were many other **city-states**. Many of the writers and philosophers that students learn about today—including Sophocles, Plato, Aristotle, and Democritus—worked during this period.

By no means did peace always remain intact through this age. Wars were often fought between city-states or between Greek alliances and an outside culture. Two of the bigger conflicts were the Persian War and the Peloponnesian War, both taking place during the 400s BCE. This last war led to the defeat of Athens and the weakening of Greece. The **Thebans**, seeing Greece's disadvantage, attacked Sparta, which had been victorious in the Peloponnesian War. Philip II of Macedon, father of Alexander the Great, entered this

The Greek god Zeus

struggle, paving the way for Greece's empire.

Phillip II was assassinated in 336 BCE, and Alexander took over his father's role. Alexander was a very capable leader, even from a young age. He had been brought up surrounded by Greek culture and taught by the philosopher Aristotle. Although he was not born Greek, he subscribed to the Greek culture. Because of his good battle command, his empire ended up stretching from Greece and Macedon, into northern Africa, and all the way to the Himalayas and the border of India. In all, his empire covered 2 million square miles.

Alexander and his army spread Greek culture throughout his empire. Greek money, art, architecture, language, myths, and other things spread out. Alexander founded several cities named after himself, which became centers of this culture.

The Hellenistic Age

The next stage of Greek history is called the Hellenistic period, considered to have begun with the death of Alexander the Great in 323 BCE. During the Hellenistic period, Greek culture became part of the fabric of people's lives in places far away from Greece. The process began under Alexander, but solidified after his death.

Over the years, city-states such as Athens attempted to revolt from the empire. These attempts earned Greece limited, but valuable results. Some southern city-states were able to gain a degree of independence from the empire. Several of these formed the Aetolian League. Unfortunately, after starting a revolt against Macedon, which controlled the empire, these city states lost their freedoms.

Roman Greece

Meanwhile, while Greece was struggling with its own wars, Rome was gaining in power. The Roman Empire eventually **annexed** Greece in 146 BCE. Roman rule did not generally affect the average Grecian. The area's culture was left alone, and local governments were allowed to function as normally as possible. Despite this freedom, Roman rule did have some impact on Greece, and city-states were required to pay **tribute** to the empire. But Greece even gained from the Romans: all free males in the empire were given the right to vote.

The Byzantine Empire

After the division of the Roman Empire, Greece became part of the Eastern, or Byzantine Empire. During this period, Greek life followed the ups and downs of the empire as a whole. Orthodox Christianity became an increasing presence, and wars were fought between the Byzantine Empire and outsiders.

During this time, the people of the Balkan Peninsula began to form a firmer idea of Gree

A Roman stadium outside Athens

identity. Although the area was relatively poor after joining the Byzantine Empire, it gained a more unified Greek way of life, including a common language and religion.

OTTOMAN RULE

In 1453 CE, the Byzantine Empire fell to the Ottomans, a Turkish group of people, and the Byzantine period ended. To avoid Ottoman rule, the Greeks took action in the

The church played on ongoing role in Greek history.

form of migration. Some traveled to Western Europe, while others moved from the plains of Greece to the mountains. The Greeks who ended up under Turkish rule resented it. Greeks often became Crypto-Christians, or those who practiced Turkish Islam but were secretly Christian. Those who actually converted to Islam were sometime **ostracized** by other Greeks who believed the new Muslims were abandoning their Greek heritage.

In 1821, the Greeks began to fight for independence. Greek culture and identity had survived and strengthened. Greeks no longer wanted to be ruled by people who were not Greek. Russia, the United Kingdom, and France eventually entered the war on the side of the Greeks. Greece fought on until 1832, when it was granted independence from Turkey. A republic was initially established but became a monarchy in 1833.

GREECE ENTERS THE MODERN WORLD

During World War I, Greece fought on the side of the Allies against the Central Powers, including

THE CAPITAL

Athens has long been an important part of Greece. From a major city-state, it has transformed into the country's capital. It is the country's economic, cultural, financial, and political center.

The city was named for Athena, the Greek goddess of wisdom. It is the site of many important examples of Greek art and architecture, including the Parthenon, the Acropolis, and the chapel of Ai Giorgis. Its many museums house Greek sculptures and paintings.

Athens is one of the most diverse places in Greece. Many of the country's immigrants, as well as millions of ethnic Greeks, call Athens home. This ethnic diversity, coupled with the culture present in Athens, makes this city a popular destination for tourists. A large portion of the local population has been provided with jobs and the city's modernization can be traced to Athens' reputation as a tourist destination.

Turkey. After the war, Greece was given small amounts of land in return for its help.

In World War II, Greece again sided with the Allied Powers, although it had little to offer with its small number of troops. Italy invaded Greece in 1940, but Greece earned the first Allied victory of World War II when it defeated Italian forces. Eventually, the Axis Powers overwhelmed Greece and occupied the country. Thousands of people were killed, some in concentration camps, others in battle. Jews were especially hunted by the occupying Germans, although the Greek Orthodox Church tried to save many.

The aftermath of World War II did not see much improvement for the Greeks. Greece's econ-

Prime minister Lucas Papademos was the head of the European Central Bank between 2002 and 2010. In 2011, he was given the task of saving his country from economic disaster.

omy had been destroyed during the war and occupation. Many Greeks believed it was time for a change in government. A civil war was fought in 1949 between royalists who supported the king and **communists**.

Greece's government during the 1960s and 1970s was anything but stable. In 1967, a **coup** overthrew the government and set up the Regime of the Colonels, which forced the king into **exile**. Many believed the United States was involved in this action. An election in 1974 disbanded the monarchy and set up a democratic constitution the following year.

GREECE TODAY

The country joined the European Union (EU) in 1981, making it a part of the European community as a whole. One of Greece's biggest moments in the last few years has been hosting the Olympic Games in 2004. Although the Olympic Games were not a financial success, they did bring new attention to this ancient country. It is now enjoying tourism and new technology that has brought Greece into the twenty-first century, despite the financial troubles it is currently dealing with.

Democracy has continued to thrive in Greece, its ancient birthplace. Today, the country's government consists of the elected president, elected for a five-year term; the 300-member parliament; and the judiciary system. Voting is universal over the age of eighteen.

Greece's economy grew throughout the last few decades, but it has recently taken a downward turn. The global financial crisis has put a damper on Greece's prosperity and success. In fact, Greece has been the hardest-hit country in Europe.

In 2011, Prime Minister Lucas Papademos, who is an **economist**, took over the leadership of Greece, replacing George Papandreou. He and other experts will lead the government, at least temporarily, in the face of economic problems, until new elections can be held. The debt crisis in Greece has affected just about everything, including politics.

Tourists flock to Greece's seaside towns, enriching the Greek economy.

CHAPTER 3 THE ECONOMY

As in most countries today, Greece's economy has been changing, shifting from agriculture, to industry, to service. For a while, the country was able to keep up with the changing world and had a stable and prosperous economy. Unfortunately, the recent global financial crisis has hit Greece especially hard. As of 2009, Greece has been in a recession, and has not yet recovered.

One of Greece's many open-air markets

The Changing Role of Agriculture and Industry

Agriculture has always been an important part of the Greek economy. However, after the mid-1900s, it began to decline because of the rise in industrial activity. While Greece used to rely almost entirely on exporting agricultural products, it now adds industrial goods to its export list. Greece produces such crops as cotton, grapes, olives, tobacco, and vegetables. Sheep and goats are two of its most important livestock outputs.

Greece began to develop its industries after World War II. This was due to foreign aid and sup-

portive government policies. Industry contributes 22 percent to Greece's **gross domestic product (GDP)**, second to the service industry. Processed foods, clothing, chemicals, and cement are Greece's primary industries. Mining is another source of Greece's exports. Bauxite, nickel, iron ore, asbestos, and marble are all found below the earth and mined extensively.

EMPLOYERS

The government provides many jobs to the Greek people. Since the government owns and runs many institutions, like banks, schools, and hospitals, it must employ people to work there. A large percentage of the people also work for businesses owned by government banks.

Those not employed by the government often work for them-selves. Traditional family businesses are still a big part of the Greek economy, as is self-employment in newer businesses. The **entrepreneurial** spirit runs high in Greece.

QUICK FACTS: THE ECONOMY OF GREECE

Gross Domestic Product (GDP): US$305.6 billion (2011 est.)
GDP per capita: US$27,600 (2011 est.)
Industries: tourism, food and tobacco processing, textiles, chemicals, metal products; mining, petroleum
Agriculture: wheat, corn, barley, sugar beets, olives, tomatoes, wine, tobacco, potatoes; beef, dairy products
Export commodities: food and beverages, manufactured goods, petroleum products, chemicals, textiles
Export partners: Germany 10.9%, Italy 10.9%, Cyprus 7.3%, Bulgaria 6.5%, Turkey 5.4%, UK 5.3%, Belgium 5.1%, China 4.8%, Switzerland 4.5%, Poland 4.2% (2010)
Import commodities: machinery, transport equipment, fuels, chemicals
Import partners: Germany 10.6%, Italy 9.9%, Russia 9.6%, China 6.1%, Netherlands 5.3%, France 4.9%, Austria 4.5% (2010)
Currency: euro
Currency exchange rate: US $1= 0.7107 euro (March, 2012)

Note: All figures are from 2011 unless otherwise noted.
Source: www.cia.gov, 2012.

Fishing is important to the Greek economy.

A Country for Tourists

The ancient history and art, as well as the beaches, of Greece have long proved to be attractive to people around the world. Tourism has provided a big boost to the Greek economy during the last few decades and now accounts for a large part of the country's GDP. The service industry, of which tourism is a part, makes up 69 percent of the GDP. Hotels have been built, local arts and crafts sold, and transportation improved to accommodate the growing number of tourists.

Transportation

Greece has a public transportation system that allows visitors and inhabitants to travel around the cities, as well as the whole country. Buses and trains are the two most popular and most extensive systems on land. Athens has a subway system as well. Ferries travel between Greece's many islands.

Greece also has a number of airports, both international and **domestic**. Olympic Airways and Aegean Airlines offer transportation between Greece's larger cities. International airports are located in Athens and Thessaloníki.

Roads in Greece are usually paved and modern. Six thousand miles (9,656 kilometers) of roads have been classified as national highways, connecting different parts of the country.

Small businesses still have their part in the Greek economy.

ENERGY

Greece's abundant coal supply provides the country with two-thirds of its energy. Greece also uses oil, but since it does not have this particular resource within its borders, it must import it. Because of its thousands of miles of coastline, Greece is able to **exploit** the energy from the sea, converting the action of the waves into hydroelectric power, which provides 6 percent of Greece's electricity.

THE DEBT CRISIS

In 2009, Greece's economy took a turn for the worse. There are several reasons for the problems Greece faces today. During the 1990s and 2000s, Greece was doing well financially. Banks and other **creditors** allowed the Greek government and people to borrow money because it seemed like a safe bet that the money would be paid off. However, people spent a lot of money, more than they could afford. The government used loans to build up the country's **infrastructure** and to improve life. Individuals bought new homes, cars, and other expensive things. In all, spending doubled in the past decade or so.

For a while, everything looked great. Then the world's economy hit a downturn. Greece couldn't cope with the new economic problems. The basic problem was that Greece was spending too much money. Its national **deficit** was enormous. In 2009, the deficit was 15 percent of Greece's GDP.

To make matters worse, people hadn't been paying their taxes; many had been practicing tax

Former Greek prime minister George Papandreou resigned in 2011 to allow a new government to save the country's economy.

evasion. The government wasn't bringing in enough money to even begin paying off its debts.

Then, a new government took over under Prime Minister George Papandreou. The new government took a look at the state that the country was in, and announced to the world that it had discovered a bigger debt than anyone had thought Greece had. To combat these problems, Greece introduced *austerity* measures. The government had to cut how much it was spending, in order to reduce the deficit. The cuts include paying government employees less, increasing taxes, raising the retirement age, and reducing *pensions*. So far, these measures are working bit by bit. In 2011, when Lucas Papademos became prime minister, Greece's deficit was reduced to 9 percent of its GDP.

Life in Greece will be tough for a long time to come. Citizens will have to get used to changes in their lifestyles so that their country can regain its economic health.

GREECE'S AUSTERITY PLAN

Some of the austerity measures include:

• public sector pay frozen until 2014.
• no bonuses for public sector employees.
• state pensions frozen or cut.
• raise in retirement age from 61 to 63.
• taxes on fuel, alcohol, and tobacco increased by 20 percent.
• new taxes on property and gambling.

The sea plays an imprtant role in Greece's culture.

4 GREECE'S PEOPLE AND CULTURE

Greece is a very **homogeneous** society; 98 percent of its citizens are ethnic Greeks, with the remaining 2 percent being mainly comprised of Turks and illegal immigrants, especially Albanians. As a result, although it lacks diversity, Greece is a unified country in which its people share a common culture.

In the 1950s and 1960s, a large number of Greeks left their country for those of Western Europe. Approximately 10 percent left their homes in Greece in order to escape the troubled times in their country. When times calmed, many returned to their homeland.

LANGUAGE

Unlike countries where there is more **diversity** in the population, most Greeks speak the same language. Modern Greek differs from the language of Ancient Greece, but they do share the same alphabet.

In addition to Greek, many people are able to speak German and English. Minorities are sometimes heard to speak Turkish, Macedonian, or Albanian.

RELIGION

Another unifying force in Greek life is the Greek Orthodox Church. Those same 98 percent of citizens who are Greek also practice this religion. Interestingly, of these people, 10 percent are Old Calendarists, meaning that they use the old Julian calendar instead of the modern Gregorian one. Islam is the next most practiced religion, followed by Roman Catholicism.

Religion plays an integral role in Greek holidays and festivals. Easter is especially important in Greek religious life, as well as the Feast of the Dormition, or Assumption.

QUICK FACTS: THE PEOPLE OF GREECE

Population: 10,767,827 (July 2012 est.)

Ethnic groups: Greek 93%, other (foreign citizens) 7% (note: percents represent citizenship, since Greece does not collect data on ethnicity)

Age structure:
  0–14 years: 14.2%
  15–64 years: 66.2%
  65 years and over: 19.6% (2011 est.)

Population growth rate: 0.06% (2012 est.)

Birth rate: 9.08 births/1,000 population (2012 est.)

Death rate: 10.8 deaths/1,000 population (July 2012 est.)

Migration rate: 2.32 migrant(s)/1,000 population (2012 est.)

Infant mortality rate: 4.92 deaths/1,000 live births

Life expectancy at birth:
  Total population: 80.05 years
  Male: 77.48 years
  Female: 82.79 years (2012 est.)

Total fertility rate: 1.39 children born/woman (2012 est.)

Religions: Greek Orthodox (official) 98%, Muslim 1.3%, other 0.7%

Languages: Greek (official) 99%, other (includes English and French) 1%

Literacy rate: 96%

Note: All figures are from 2011 unless otherwise noted.
Source: www.cia.gov, 2012.

Christianity is important to Greece's cultural life.

Greek cuisine

EUROPEAN UNION—GREECE

MUSLIMS IN THE EUROPEAN UNION

Muslims are people who follow Islam, a religion that grew from some of the same roots as Judaism and Christianity. "Islam" means "submission to God," and Muslims try to let God shape all aspects of their lives. They refer to God as Allah; their holy scriptures are called the Qur'an, and they consider the Prophet Muhammad to be their greatest teacher.

About 16 million Muslims live in the European Union—but their stories vary from country to country. Some Muslim populations have been living in Europe for hundreds of years. Others came in the middle of the twentieth century. Still others are recent refugees from the troubled Middle East. By 2020, the Muslim population in Europe is predicted to double. By 2050, one in five Europeans are likely to be Muslim, and by 2100, Muslims may make up one-quarter of Europe's people.

Not all Europeans are happy about these predictions. Negative stereotypes about Muslims are common in many EU countries. Some Europeans think all Muslims are terrorists. But stereotypes are dangerous!

When you believe a stereotype, you think that people in a certain group all act a certain way. "All jocks are dumb" is a stereotype. "All women are emotional" is another stereotype, and another is, "All little boys are rough and noisy." Stereotypes aren't true! And when we use stereotypes to think about others, we often fall into prejudice—thinking that some groups of people aren't as good as others.

Fundamentalist Muslims want to get back to the fundamentals—the basics—of Islam. However, their definition of what's "fundamental" is not always the same as other Muslims'. Generally speaking, they are afraid that the influence of Western morals and values will be bad for Muslims. They believe that the laws of Islam's holy books should be followed literally. Many times, they are willing to kill for their beliefs—and they are often willing to die for them as well. Men and women who are passionate about these beliefs have taken part in violent attacks against Europe and the United States. They believe that terrorism will make the world take notice of them, that it will help them fight back against the West's power.

But most Muslims are not terrorists. In fact, most Muslims are law-abiding and hardworking citizens of the countries where they live. Some Muslims, however, believe that women should have few of the rights that women expect in most countries of the EU. This difference creates tension, since the EU guarantees women the same rights as men.

But not all Muslims are so conservative and strict. Many of them believe in the same "golden rule" preached by all major religions: "Treat everyone the way you want to be treated."

But despite this, hate crimes against Muslims are increasing across the EU. These crimes range from death threats and murder to more minor assaults, such as spitting and name-calling. Racism against Muslims is a major problem in many parts of the EU. The people of the European Union must come to terms with the fact that Muslims are a part of them now. Terrorism is the enemy to be fought—not Muslims.

The ruins of ancient Greek architecture

EDUCATION

Greeks place much importance on education and work hard to provide a good education for students. School attendance is **compulsory** until age fourteen, when it becomes optional to continue. It is free at all times. Students who continue their education tend to get better jobs in Greece, since many employers require their workers to have had attended school past the age of fourteen.

There are no private universities, so competition for acceptance is tight for those wanting to attend the small number of public universities. Some students attend unofficial private schools that offer higher education or study outside of Greece.

SPORTS: THE EFFECTS OF THE OLYMPICS

True to their history of hosting the original Olympic Games, Greeks continue to participate in sports. Soccer (or football, as it's called in Europe) and basketball are popular. The popularity of basketball is very unusual, since it is not so prominent in other European countries.

At the Olympics themselves, Greece has reason to be proud. It hosted the first modern Olympics in 1896 and has since produced many medal-winning athletes. In 2004, Athens again hosted the Olympics, and many stadiums and other accommodations were built especially for the games. Athens now has state-of-the-art sports facilities, although not necessarily anyone to use them.

Hosting the 2004 Summer Olympics proved to be very costly. Estimates place the cost of the Olympics at $10 or even $15 billion. In fact, the bill, which was footed mostly by the government, added to Greece's current debt crisis.

FOOD

From cafes to restaurants, Greeks love to eat their favorite foods out of their own kitchens. Cafes, or *kafeneias*, are popular places to eat pastries or drink a cup of coffee. Once they were open only to men, but that is now changing. Other places, like tavernas, are informal restaurants suitable for eating a full meal.

In restaurants and at home, Greek cuisine shows the influence that Turkey has had on the country. *Souvlaki* (meat in pita bread), *tzatziki* (cucumber and yogurt dip), and *spanikopita* (spinach in filo dough) are traditional dishes of Turkish origin. Desserts include *baklava* and *kadayifi*, both made with large amounts of honey, typical in most desserts.

LITERATURE: PAST AND PRESENT

Many of Greece's writers are famous in the Western world, and their works, often referred to as the Classics. Many are required reading in school. The most well known, Homer, wrote *The Iliad* and *The Odyssey*. Other writers include the poet Sappho, who wrote love poems, and Pausanias, the world's first travel writer.

Although Greek literature is often dominated by the writers of ancient times, the country also

The ancient Greeks were skilled sculptors.

boasts well-written modern works. Two Greek poets, Odysseus Elytis and George Seferis, won the Nobel Prize for literature during the 1900s. Other writers, such as novelist Nikos Kazantzakis, are famous in Greece and becoming better known in other parts of the world.

ART AND ARCHITECTURE

Throughout the long history of Greece, the art of the area has changed with the age and with the people. Greek art even directly influenced Roman art forms. Sculptures of ancient Greece often depicted human figures or myths. One theme that has remained the same is the Greeks' love of painted pottery, with designs ranging from figures to geometric patterns.

Few examples remain of Ancient Greek architecture; what have survived are mostly temples such as the Temple of Hephaestus and the Parthenon, created by the Greek architect Iktinos.

Additionally, many theaters, which were important centers in towns, have survived.

Greek art is not all ancient. More modern artists include El Greco (Domenikos Theotokopoulos) from the island of Crete, who spent most of his life painting in Spain during the 1500s. Even more recently, artists such as painters Constantine Andreou, Giorgio de Chirico, Jannis Kounellis, and Theodoros Stamos have come out of Greece.

MUSIC AND DANCE

Traditional forms of music tend to be popular among Greeks, even with the younger generations. One such example is *rebetika* music, which contains messages about suffering and poverty.

Dances often accompany music, especially at family celebrations and events. The *hasapiko*, *kalamatiano*, and *tsamiko* are all common Greek dances. As in other areas of culture, dances show traditions imported from Turkey.

Sounio, Greece

5 LOOKING TO THE FUTURE

Greece's future is very uncertain. Nobody knows how long it will take the country to recover from its current economic woes. It will be a long struggle, though, with no easy answers, and that struggle will affect plenty of other European countries.

While it is recovering, Greece must rely on help from other members of the EU. Taxpayers from other more stable nations such as France and Germany have had to supply the money for Greece's bailout loans.

Even if Greece can move past its most immediate problems, the country will still have things to worry about. Investors probably still won't want to put their money into Greece. They will worry that Greece won't be able to pay them back.

The Euro

The problems in Greece could spell out the beginning of the end for the euro. Currently, seventeen members of the EU use the common currency of the euro. Altogether, these countries form the Eurozone. The euro was introduced in 1999 and was meant to unify the EU even further. Today, over 330 million people use euros every day.

The history of the euro isn't very long in Greece. The Greek government had worked hard to introduce it to the country, forcing the high inflation rate down and increasing taxes. Despite these unpopular policies, Greece was unable to meet the qualifications to adopt the euro. Greece continued working toward acceptance of the euro and finally met the goal set by the EU in 2000. The euro was then put into circulation in 2001.

Some people are afraid that Greece will now leave the Eurozone. It might be better for Greece

Economists around the world fear that economic problems in nations like Greece, Spain, Portugal and others may strain the European Union. Some even fear that the recession that began in 2008 will eventually lead to the end of the eurozone.

Tourists from around the world travel to Greece to see the nation's amazing ancient architechture.

itself to do that; it could help the country pay off its debts. However, it wouldn't be so good for the rest of the Eurozone. Other EU members are having the same problems as Greece, although on a smaller scale. Portugal and Spain, along with Italy and Ireland, all have debt problems that are being made worse by the global financial crisis. These other countries might decide to the same thing, and eventually the euro would just collapse.

No one's really sure what's going to happen. While some analysts are raising the alarm, others claim that the euro is just fine and that there's nothing to worry about. The EU has so far been committed to keeping the Eurozone intact.

GREECE'S FUTURE

One major bright spot for Greece is tourism. People still want to visit the country's ancient sites and beautiful coasts. So far, they aren't letting the country's financial problems get in the way.

Tourism is continuing to increase, as foreign visitors pour into Greece. The debt crisis doesn't affect the average tourist, who still has plenty of money to spend on hotels, dinners, boating tours, and other things. Tourists bring in money and make sure that jobs are still available for those who need them. Tourism could help Greece recover more quickly, and get back on its feet.

Greece's recovery will be based partly on how the rest of the EU is doing. Other countries are teetering on the edge of their own crises, although so far, none are as serious as Greece's.

Will Greece's economic problems lead to its leaving the eurozone, or even the EU altogether?

Will Greece be able to repay its loans? Will it leave the euro behind? Will the Greek people continue to lose jobs and security? Only time will tell. And it will depend on the EU's ability to work together to help a member in need.

THE MEMBERS OF THE EUROZONE ARE:

Austria
Belgium
Cyprus
Estonia
Finland
France
Germany
Greece
Ireland
Italy
Luxembourg
Malta
The Netherlands
Portugal
Slovakia
Slovenia
Spain

TIME LINE

3000 BCE	The Minoans arrive in Greece.
1600 BCE	Mycenaeans invade Greece; the Bronze Age begins.
1100 BCE	The Bronze Age ends.
1100–700 BCE	The Dark Ages envelop Greece.
776 BCE	The first Olympic Games are held.
497–479 BCE	The Persian Wars are fought.
461–445 BCE	The first Peloponnesian War occurs.
431–404 BCE	The second Peloponnesian War is fought.
323 BCE	Alexander the Great dies.
146 BCE	Greece is annexed into the Roman Empire.
395 CE	The Byzantine Empire is formed.
1453	The Byzantine Empire falls to the Ottomans.
1812	The Greeks begin to fight for independence.
1829	The Greeks win their independence from the Turks.

1940	Italy invades Greece.
1949	The Greek civil war is fought.
1967	The Regime of the Colonels begins.
1974	An election leads to the disbanding of the monarchy.
1975	A democratic constitution goes into effect.
1981	Greece joins the EU.
2001	Greece adopts the euro.
2004	Greece hosts the Summer Olympics.
2008	The world faces a global recession.
2009	Greece's economy goes into recession. George Papandreou becomes prime minister.
2011	Lucas Papademos becomes prime minister.

Further Reading/Internet Resources

Greenblatt, Miriam. *Alexander the Great and Ancient Greece.* New York: Benchmark Books, 2000.

Heinrichs, Ann, and Amy J. Johnson. *Greece.* New York: Scholastic Library, 2001.

Nardo, Don. *Ancient Greece.* Farmington Hills, Mich.: Gale Group, 2000.

Nardo, Don. *Women of Ancient Greece.* San Diego, Calif.: Lucent.

Travel Information

www.greek-tourism.gr

History and Geography

www.ancientgreece.com

www.historyforkids.org

Culture and Festivals

www.lonelyplanet.com/destinations/europe/greece/culture.htm

www1.greece.gr/ABOUT_GREECE/CountryProfile/about_profile_Cultural_Life%20.htm

Economic and Political Information
earthtrends.wri.org/text/economics-business/country-profile-73.html
www.hri.org/cgi-bin/brief?/nodes/grpol.html

EU Information
europa.eu.int

Publisher's note:
The websites listed on this page were active at the time of publication. The publisher is not responsible for websites that have changed their addresses or discontinued operation since the date of publication. The publisher will review and update the website list upon each reprint.

FOR MORE INFORMATION

Consulate General of Greece
69 East 79th Street
New York, NY 10021
Tel.: 212-988-5500

Embassy of Greece
2221 Massachusetts Avenue NW
Washington, DC 20008
Tel.: 202-939-5800

Embassy of the United States
91 Vasilissis Sophias Avenue
Athens 10160 Greece
Tel.: 30-210-721-2951

U.S. Department of State
2201 C Street NW
Washington, DC 20520
Tel.: 202-642-4000

GLOSSARY

annexed: Took over territory and incorporated it into another political body.

archaeologists: Scientists who study ancient cultures through the examination of their material remains.

austerity: A plan for reduced government spending that often means the public had to do without many services.

autonomous: Politically independent and self-governing.

Bronze Age: A historical period between 3500 and 1500 BCE, characterized by the use of tools made of bronze.

capital: Wealth in the form of property or money.

city-states: Independent states consisting of a sovereign city and its surrounding territory.

communists: Supporters of the political and economic theory in which all property and wealth is owned by all the members of a community.

compulsory: Required.

coup: The sudden overthrow of a government and seizure of political power.

creditors: People who loan money.

deficit: Lack; the difference between what is needed and what's actually there.

diversity: A variety of something.

domestic: Produced, distributed, sold, or occurring within a country.

economist: Someone who studies everything that has to do with money in a particular country.

entrepreneurial: Relating to the setting up and financing of a commercial enterprise.

epics: Lengthy narrative poems.

evasion: The process of staying away from something else.

exile: Forced to live in another country.

exploit: Use, take advantage of.

gross domestic product (GDP): The total value of all goods and services produced within a country in a year, minus net income from investments in other countries.

homogeneous: Consisting of the same kind of elements.

infrastructure: Roads, telephone lines, and other services that allow a country to function.

intricacy: Complex, with many details.

ostracized: Refused to associate with someone so that he or she is kept separate from the rest of the group.

pensions: Payments made during retirement.

Phoenicians: Members of an ancient people who occupied Phoenicia, in present-day Syria.

prehistoric: Relating to the period before history was first recorded in writing.

recession: A period of economic slowdown.

solidarity: To stand together in unity.

tariff: A government-imposed tax on imports.

Thebans: Those who lived in the ancient Greek city of Thebes, north-west of present-day Athens.

tribute: Payment made by one ruler or state to another as a sign of submission.

INDEX

agriculture 28
Alexander the Great 19, 20
Ancient Greece 17, 18, 19
architecture 45
Aristotle 19, 20
art 45
Athens 19, 23
austerity 35

Byzantine Empire 20, 21

Christianity 21, 38
culture 37–45

dance 45
dating systems 18
debt 33, 35, 51

economy 25, 27–35, 48
education 41
energy 33
European Economic Community 12
euro 48
EU
       formation 12
       Greek membership 25
eurozone 48, 51

food 41
France 23

gross domestic product (GDP) 28, 31, 35

Hellenistic Greek 20
Homer 18

independence (Greek) 23

language 38
literature 41, 45

Minoans 17, 18
music 45
Muslims (Islam) 23
Mycenaeans 17, 18, 41

Olympic Games 25, 41
Ottomans 23

Papademos, Lucas 24, 35
Papandreou, George 25, 34, 35
Peloponnesian War 19
Persian War 19
Philip of Macedon 19, 20
philosophers 19
prehistoric Greece 17

recession 13
Rome 20

Thebans 19
tourism 31, 51
transportation 31
Turkey 23

unemployment 15
United Kingdom 23
United States 25

World War I 23
World War II 12, 23, 25, 28

PICTURE CREDITS

Erichui | Dreamstime.com: p. 10
Author's Image: p. 28, 30, 32, 36–37, 40, 42, 44
Corel: p. 16–17, 26–27
Kpikoulas | Dreamstime.com: p. 14
Lefteris Papaulakis | Dreamstime.com: p. 46
P00p | Dreamstime.com: p. 13
Photos.com: p. 19, 21, 22, 39, 50
Rottovi | Dreamstime.com: p. 49
Vasilis Filis: p. 34
Yong hian Lim | Dreamstime.com: p. 52

All other images are from Corel Image Collections, except those that are in the public domain. If any image has been inadvertently uncredited, please notify Harding House Publishing Services, Vestal, New York 13850, so that rectification can be made for future printings.

About the Author and the Consultant

Author

Kim Etingoff currently lives in Boston, Massachusetts. She grew up in New York State and graduated from the University of Rochester. She has since been pursuing her interests in sustainable farming, nutrition, and writing.

Series Consultant

Ambassador John Bruton served as Irish Prime Minister from 1994 until 1997. As prime minister, he helped turn Ireland's economy into one of the fastest-growing in the world. He was also involved in the Northern Ireland Peace Process, which led to the 1998 Good Friday Agreement. During his tenure as Ireland's prime minister, he also presided over the European Union presidency in 1996 and helped finalize the Stability and Growth Pact, which governs management of the euro. Before being named the European Commission Head of Delegation in the United States, he was a member of the convention that drafted the European Constitution, signed October 29, 2004.

The European Commission Delegation to the United States represents the interests of the European Union as a whole, much as ambassadors represent their countries' interests to the U.S. government. Matters coming under European Commission authority are negotiated between the commission and the U.S. administration.